Twenty to Make
Crocheted Beanies

Frauke Kiedaisch

Search Press

First published in Great Britain 2013

Search Press Limited
Wellwood, North Farm Road,
Tunbridge Wells, Kent, TN2 3DR

Reprinted 2014

The original German edition was published
as *Be Beanie!*

Copyright © 2012 frechverlag GmbH, Stuttgart,
Germany (www.frech.de)

This edition is published by arangement with
Claudia Böhme Rights & Literary Agency,
Hannover, Germany (www.agency-boehme.com)

Photos: frechverlag GmbH, 70499 Stuttgart;
lichtpunkt, Michael Ruder, Stuttgart;
Esther Saathoff
Make-up: Diekmann Face Art, Ludwigsburg

English translation by
Burravoe Translation Services

Print ISBN: 978-1-78221-000-9
Epub ISBN: 978-1-78126-196-5
Mobi ISBN: 978-1-78126-197-2
PDF ISBN: 978-1-78126-198-9

Printed in China

Terminology and hook sizes

Metric, US and UK hook sizes are provided
in this book. In the patterns themselves,
both UK and US crochet terminology has
been provided – the US terms are given first,
followed by the UK terms in brackets.

For all abbreviations used in this book, and
UK and US crochet term conversions, refer
to the key on the book flaps.

Publisher's Note
If you would like more information about
crocheting, try the
Beginner's Guide to Crochet
by Pauline Turner, Search Press, 2005.

Contents

Introduction
Hints and Tips 6

Cool Classic 8
Sailor Girl 10
Baker Boy 12
All That Glitters 14
Fibre Fun 16
Pretty in Pink 18
Hippy Chic 20
Dream Weave 22
Lady Grey 24

Colour Clash 26
Starry, Starry Night 28
Flirty Flowers 30
Colour Fun 32
Light and Lacy 34
Making Waves 36
Filet Fun 38
Shades of Grey 40
Winter Wonder 42
Chic Black and White 44
Street Smart 46

Yarn Information 48

Introduction

Beanies are a must-have all year round, whatever the weather. This book includes one for every taste or occasion – sporty or glamorous, feminine or funky, lightweight or chunky – and best of all, these fashionable hats can be crocheted quickly, even by relative beginners. In fact, all the patterns are suitable for beginners or intermediate crocheters. Don't be afraid of the charts – these actually make it easier to follow the patterns, helping you see at a glance what each design looks like and where you are in the pattern.

The great thing about crocheting beanies is their versatility, and this is exactly why they are so much fun to make. So, pick up your crochet hook and enjoy making one of the beanies from this book – once you've made one, you're bound to be hooked and will want to make another!

Hints and Tips

You will notice that some of the project instructions refer to the crochet stitches section on the book flaps. There you will find step-by-step instructions and photographs to guide you through some of the more detailed techniques.

Before starting, read through these simple tips below:

Yarn selection

For best results, use the specific yarns listed with each project and always make a tension (gauge) swatch. When using alternative yarns, make sure you can achieve the same tension. On page 48 you will find detailed information on the specific yarns that were used in this book.

Tension (gauge) sample

This is usually worked to make a 10 x 10cm (4 x 4in) square and states the number of stitches for the width and the number of rows for the height using the recommended hook size. For accuracy, work a few extra stitches and rows, stretch out your sample and then count how many rows and stitches are required to make a piece 10 x 10cm (4 x 4in) square.

Working in rounds

Most of the beanies are worked in rounds starting at the crown. You can begin with a chain foundation ring, which leaves a decorative hole in the centre, or, if there is to be only a small hole or no hole, begin with two chain stitches. See the instructions on the book flaps for both these methods.

Street Smart
Crochet pattern for page 46

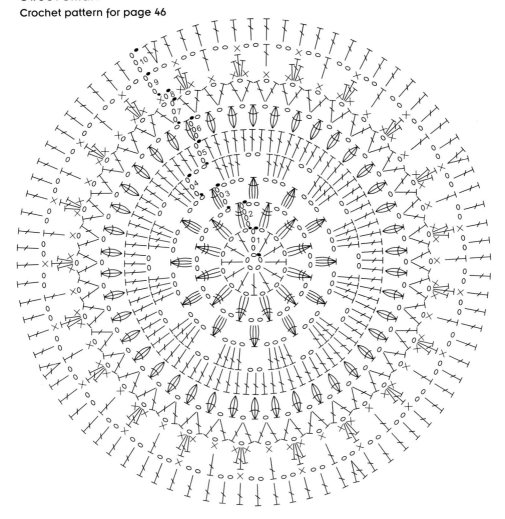

Cool Classic

Size:
Head circumference 54–58cm (21¼–23in)

Materials:
2 x 50g (1¾oz) balls of SMC Select Apiretto
  yarn or similar Aran-weight yarn in navy blue
  (8106)
Crochet hook, size 6mm (US J/10, UK 4)

Tension sample:
12 sts and 6 rounds of dc (*UK tr*) using the
6.0mm (US J/10, UK 4) crochet hook
= 10 x 10cm (4 x 4in).
Change your hook if necessary to obtain the
correct tension (gauge).

Making a bobble:
The band around the beanie has a decorative
bobble pattern. Work each bobble as follows:

Bobble: * yrh, insert your hook in the st, yrh and
draw through 1 loop * , rep from * to * twice
more, yrh, insert your hook in the st, yrh and
draw through all 9 loops on the hook.

Basic pattern:
Work rounds 1–5 following the chart to
work dc (*UK tr*) and ch in rounds in the
shape of an octagon. Start every round
with 1 dc (*UK tr*) (counts as 3 ch) and 1 ch
and join up with a sl st into the 3rd ch of
the start of the round. Count the 1st 3 ch
of the start of the round as the last dc (*UK
tr*) of each round. The numbers show the
round transitions. The first 5 rounds are
shown in full.

Double crochet together:
See the crochet stitches guide on the book flaps.

Instructions:
Start the beanie at the crown and work down to
the bottom edge in rounds as explained below.
This will create the octagonal shape.

Begin with 4 ch and join into a ring with a sl st.

Round 1: Work 3 ch (counts as 1st dc/*UK tr*),
then alternate 1 ch, 1 dc (*UK tr*) as shown.

Rounds 2–5: Work following the
crochet pattern.

Rounds 6–12: Rep round 5, alternating 9 dc (*UK
tr*), 1 ch, and working without increases. Make
the round transition as for round 5
[80 sts per round].

Round 13: 1 ch then sc2tog (*UK dc2tog*) to end
of round; join with a sl st [40 sts].

Round 14: 1 ch then sc (*UK dc*) into every st
around; join with a sl st [40 sts].

Round 15: 1 ch, work * 1 sc (*UK dc*), 1 bobble * ,
rep from * to * to end of round, join with a sl st.

Round 16: Rep round 14.

Fasten off all yarns carefully.

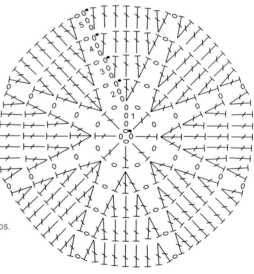

Sailor Girl

Size:
Head circumference 54–58cm (21¼–23in)

Materials:
1 x 50g (1¾oz) ball of Regia Color 6-ply yarn
  or similar sport-weight/sock yarn in each of
  cherry (2002) and marine blue (0324)
Crochet hook, size 5mm (US H/8, UK 6)

Tension sample:
17 sts and 22 rounds of sc (UK dc) using the
5mm (US H/8, UK 6) crochet hook
= 10 x 10cm (4 x 4in). Change your hook
if necessary to obtain the correct
tension (gauge).

Colour pattern:
Rounds 1–40: Crochet alternately 4 rounds in
cherry, 4 rounds in marine blue. When changing
colour, draw in the new colour on the last st of
the previous round to achieve a perfect colour
transition (see the crochet stitches guide on the
book flaps).
Rounds 41–50: Crochet alternately 2 rounds in
cherry, 2 rounds in marine blue.

Sc (UK dc) in spiral rounds:
Work sc (UK dc) in rounds like spirals, marking
the start of the round with a contrasting thread
(see the crochet stitches guide on the book
flaps).

Instructions:
Start the beanie at the crown and work down to
the bottom edge in spiral rounds of sc (UK dc)
as explained here.

Begin with 2 ch in cherry.

Round 1: Work 6 sc (UK dc) into the 2nd ch
from the hook (see the crochet stitches guide
on the book flaps). Mark the start of the row
with contrasting yarn.

Round 2 (cherry): 2 sc (UK dc) in every st
around [12 sts].

Round 3 (cherry): Work * 1 sc (UK dc) then 2 sc
(UK dc) in next st * , rep from * to * around
[18 sts].

Round 4 (cherry): Work * sc (UK dc) in each of
next 2 sts then 2 sc (UK dc) in next st * , rep
from * to * around [24 sts].

Round 5 (blue): Work * sc (UK dc) in each of
next 3 sts then 2 sc (UK dc) in next st * , rep
from * to * around [30 sts].

Round 6 (blue): Work * sc (UK dc) in each of
next 4 sts then 2 sc (UK dc) in next st * , rep
from * to * around [36 sts].

Round 7 (blue): Work * sc (UK dc) in each of
next 5 sts then 2 sc (UK dc) in next st * , rep
from * to * around [42 sts].

Round 8 (blue): Work sc (UK dc) in every st
around [42 sts].

Round 9 (cherry): Work * sc (UK dc) in each of
next 6 sts then 2 sc (UK dc) in next st * , rep
from * to * around [48 sts].

Round 10 (cherry): Work * sc (UK dc) in each
of next 7 sts then 2 sc (UK dc) in next st * , rep
from * to * around [54 sts].

Round 11 (cherry): Work * sc (UK dc) in each
of next 8 sts then 2 sc (UK dc) in next st * , rep
from * to * around [60 sts].

Round 12 (cherry): Work sc (UK dc) in every st
around [60 sts].

Continue increasing in this way until the end of
round 24, changing colour after every 4 rounds
and not making any increases on the last round
of each colour. Round 24 has 114 sts.

Round 25 (cherry): Work * sc (UK dc) in each of
next 18 sts then 2 sc (UK dc) in next st * , rep
from * to * around [120 sts].

Rounds 26–39: Work sc (UK dc) in every st
around [120 sts].

Round 40 (blue): Work * sc, sc2tog (UK dc,
dc2tog) * , rep from * to * around [80 sts].

Rounds 41–45: From now on, alternate colours
every 2 rounds. Work sc (UK dc) in every st
around [80 sts].

Round 46 (cherry): Work * sc (*UK dc*) in each of the next 6 sts then sc2tog (*UK dc2tog*) * , rep from * to * around [70 sts].

Rounds 47–48 (blue): Work sc (*UK dc*) in every st around [70 sts].

Round 49 (cherry): Work sc (*UK dc*) in every st around then join into a round with a sl st.

Round 50: Still using cherry, work into each st around in rev sc (*UK rev dc*) as explained in the crochet stitches guide on the book flaps.

Baker Boy

Size:
Head circumference 54–58cm (21¼–23in)

Materials:
1 x 100g (3½oz) ball of Rowan Big Wool or similar super-bulky/chunky merino yarn in lichen green (49)

Crochet hook, size 10mm (US N/15, UK 000)

Crochet stitch marker (optional)

Tension sample:
7.5 rose double (UK treble) shells and 5.5 rounds using the 10mm (US N/15, UK 000) crochet hook = 10 x 10cm (4 x 4in). Change your hook if necessary to obtain the correct tension (gauge).

Rose double shells (rds) (UK rose treble shells, rts):
The hat is worked in spiral rounds of rose double (*UK treble*) shell. The stitch is not difficult – it begins like double crochet (*UK treble crochet*) but is finished slightly differently.

Rose double (*UK treble*) shell: yrh, insert the hook into the st, yrh, draw through 2 loops (2 loops remaining on hook), yrh, draw through the 2 remaining loops.

(NB: The design is formed only in the RS rows or rounds.)

Instructions:
Start the cap at the crown and work down to the bottom edge in spiral rounds using rds (*UK rts*).

Begin with 2 ch.

Round 1: Crochet 6 rds (*UK rts*) into the 2nd ch from the hook (see the crochet stitches guide on the book flaps). Mark the start of the round with a contrasting yarn or crochet stitch marker.

Round 2: Work 2 rds (*UK rts*) into each st around [12 sts].

Round 3: Rep round 2 [24 sts].

Round 4: Work * 1 rds (*UK rts*) then work 2 rds (*UK rts*) into the next st * , rep from * to * around [36 sts].

Round 5: Work * 1 rds (*UK rts*) into each of the next 2 sts then work 2 rds (*UK rts*) into the next st * , rep from * to * around [48 sts].

Rounds 6–10: Work 1 rds (*UK rts*) into each st around [48 sts]

Round 11: Work sc2tog (*UK dc2tog*) in every st around [24 sts].

Round 12: Working into the back loop of each st only, work sc (*UK dc*) in every st around then join into a round with a sl st. Cut the yarn.

For the peak (visor) work over 5 rows, as follows. After the 6th st along from the centre back, join in your yarn with a sl st and crochet over the next 12 sts as follows:

Row 1: 1 ch, working into the back loop of each st only, sc (*UK dc*) into each of the next 12 sts.

Rows 2–4: Work back and forth in sc (*UK dc*), working into the back loops only as before [12 sts].

Row 5: Still working in the back loops only, work 1 ch, skip the 1st st, sc (*UK dc*) into each of the next 9 sts, skip the next st, then sc (*UK dc*) into the final st. This rounds off the front.

Making up:
Work around the whole peak (visor) in sl st, working 5 sl sts along the right-side edge, 10 sl sts along the front and then 5 sl sts on the left edge.

Tip:
If you do not like peaked caps, simply leave out the last five rows and wear the hat as a cool beret.

All That Glitters

Size:
Head circumference 54–58cm (21¼–23in)

Materials:
2 x 50g (1¾oz) balls of Schachenmayr SMC
Alpaca or similar DK yarn in camel (4)

1 x 25g (1oz) ball of Anchor Artiste Metallic Fine
crochet thread in gold (300)

Crochet hooks, size 5mm (US H/8, UK 6) and
6mm (US J/10, UK 4)

Tension sample:
16 sts and 9 rounds in the basic pattern using
the 6mm (US J/10, UK 4) crochet hook
= 10 x 10cm (4 x 4in). Change your hook if
necessary to obtain the correct tension (gauge).

Basic pattern:
Crochet following the crochet pattern using a
6.0mm (US J/10, UK 4) hook and working with 2
yarns at the same time (1 yarn in camel, 1 yarn
in gold). Work the 1st – 6th rounds once, then
continue repeating the crochet pattern for the
5th and 6th rounds. Every round ends with 1
sl st into the 3rd or 1st ch from the start of the
round, see the crochet pattern below.

Instructions:
Start the beanie at the crown and work down to
the bottom edge in the basic pattern following
the chart.

Using the 2 yarns together and the 6mm (US
J/10, UK 4) hook, begin with 4 ch and join into a
ring with a sl st (see the crochet stitches on the
book flaps).

Round 1: Begin with 5 ch (1st 3 ch represent the
1st dc [UK tr]). Then work * 1dc (UK tr), 2 ch * ,
rep from * to * 6 times and join with a sl st to
the 3rd ch from the start of the round.

Rounds 2–6: Follow the chart, working the dc
(UK tr) or sc (UK dc) into the gaps under the
ch sts of the previous round. Start every round
with the appropriate number of ch as shown: 3
ch replaces the 1st dc (UK tr); 1 ch replaces the
1st sc (UK dc). The numbers show the round
transitions.

Round 7 onwards: Rep rounds 5–6 until
the piece measure 27cm (10½in) from the
foundation ch with a 6th pattern round.

Hat band: Change to the 5mm (US H/8, UK 6)
hook and 2 strands of the gold yarn, and work
1 sc (UK dc) into each dc (UK tr) and each ch
of the previous round. Work 3 more rounds,
working sc (UK dc) into each st around. Finish
the final round with a sl st into the 1st st of the
round. Fasten off all yarn ends neatly.

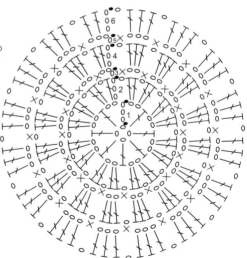

Fibre Fun

Size:
Head circumference 54–58cm (21¼–23in)

Materials:
1 x 50g (1¾oz) ball of Schachenmayr SMC Sheila Soft Mini or similar super bulky novelty yarn in toffee brown (111)

1 x 50g (1¾oz) ball of Schachenmayr SMC Extra Merino Big or similar bulky woollen yarn in dark brown (111)

Crochet hooks, sizes 5mm (US H/8, UK 6) and 8mm (US L/11, UK 0)

Tension sample:
9 sts and 9 rounds of sc (*UK dc*) using the 8.0mm (US L/11, UK 0) hook and Sheila Soft Mini yarn = 10 x 10cm (4 x 4in). Change your hook if necessary to obtain the correct tension (gauge).

Working in spiral rounds:
Work sc (*UK dc*) in rounds like spirals, without joining the last stitch of the round to the first stitch in the usual way. Mark the start of the row with a contrasting thread (see crochet stitches guide on the book flaps).

NB: Crochet the sc (*UK dc*) loosely and before each insertion of the hook, slightly open the next st with the left thumb and index finger. This will make the fluffy stitches more visible.

Working tr (UK dtr):
The flower's petals are worked in treble crochet (*UK double treble*). This long stitch is worked as follows:

Tr (*UK dtr*): yrh twice, insert the hook into the st, yrh and draw through 1 loop (4 loops on hook), yrh and draw through 2 loops (3 loops on hook), yrh and draw through 2 loops (2 loops on hook), yrh and draw through remaining 2 loops.

Instructions:
Start the beanie at the crown and work down to the bottom edge in spiral rounds of sc (*UK dc*).

Begin with 2 ch in Sheila Soft Mini using the 8.0mm (US L/11, UK 0) crochet hook.

Round 1: Work 6 sc (*UK dc*) into the 2nd ch from the hook (see the crochet stitches guide on the book flaps). Mark the start of the round with a contrasting yarn.

Round 2: Work 2 sc (*UK dc*) into every st around [12 sts].

Round 3: Work * 1 sc (*UK dc*) then work 2 sc (*UK dc*) into the next st * , rep from * to * around [18 sts].

Round 4: Work * sc (*UK dc*) into each of next 2 sts then 2 sc (*UK dc*) into next st * , rep from * to * around [24 sts].

Round 5: Work * sc (*UK dc*) into each of next 3 sts then 2 sc (*UK dc*) into next st * , rep from * to * around [30 sts].

Round 6: Work * sc (*UK dc*) into each of next 4 sts then 2 sc (*UK dc*) into next st * , rep from * to * around [36 sts].

Round 7: Work * sc (*UK dc*) into each of next 5 sts then 2 sc (*UK dc*) into next st * , rep from * to * around [42 st].

Round 8: Work * sc (*UK dc*) into each of next 6 sts then 2 sc (*UK dc*) into next st * , rep from * to * around [48 sts].

Round 9: Work * sc (*UK dc*) into each of next 7 sts then 2 sc (*UK dc*) into next st * , rep from * to * around [54 sts].

Rounds 10–20: Work sc (*UK dc*) into every st around [54 sts].

Rounds 21–26 (hat band): Change to the 5mm (US H/8, UK 6) crochet hook and Extra Merino Big yarn and continue in spiral rounds. This yarn and hook change will automatically make the edge narrower. Finish the final round with a sl st into the 1st st of the round.

Crochet flowers:

Using Extra Merino Big yarn and the 5mm (US H/8, UK 6) crochet hook, ch 5 and join into a ring with a sl st.

Round 1: 1 ch, work 16 sc (*UK dc*) into the ring then join into a round with a sl st [16 sts].

Round 2: Crochet 1 petal into every 2nd st of the previous round by working 1 sc (*UK dc*),

4 ch, 3 tr (*UK dtr*), 4 ch, 1 sc (*UK dc*) all into the same st. Work 8 petals in the round. Close the round with a sl st.

Attach the flower to the side of the finished hat, using the photograph as a guide to positioning.

Pretty in Pink

Size:
Head circumference 54–58cm (21¼–23in)

Materials:
1 x 25g (1oz) ball of Rowan Kidsilk Haze or similar lace-weight yarn in Candy Girl pink (606)

Crochet hook, size 6mm (US J/10, UK 4)

Tension sample:
11 sts and 10 rounds in hdc (UK htr) using Rowan Kidsilk Haze = 10 x 10cm (4 x 4in). Change your hook if necessary to obtain the correct tension (gauge).

Working tr (UK dtr):
See page 16 for instructions on working tr (UK dtr) for the flower petals.

Basic pattern:
Crochet spiral rounds of staggered hdc (UK htr), working very loosely. To work staggered hdc (UK htr), instead of putting the hook into the st of the previous round, put it between 2 hdc (UK htr) of the previous round, then work the hdc (UK htr) as normal. Mark the start of each round with a contrasting yarn. This will produce the mesh effect.

Crochet flower:
Work 5 ch using double yarn and join into a ring with a sl st. Work 1 ch at the start of the round, then for each petal work * 1 sc (UK dc), 3 ch, 3 htr (UK dtr), crochet 3 ch into the ring * . Rep from * to * 6 more times to make 7 petals. Close up the round with a sl st into the 1st ch of the round.

Attach the flower to the side of the finished hat, using the photograph as a guide to positioning.

Instructions:
Start the beanie at the crown and work down to the bottom edge in spiral rounds.

Begin with 2 ch.

Round 1: Work 8 hdc (UK htr) into the 2nd ch from the hook. Mark the start of the round with a contrasting yarn and continue working in spirals of staggered hdc (UK htr).

Round 2: work 2 hdc (UK htr) into each st around [16 sts].

Round 3: Work * 1 hdc (UK htr) then work 2 hdc (UK htr) into the next st * , rep from * to * around [24 sts].

Round 4: Work * 1 hdc (UK htr) into each of the next 2 sts, then 2 hdc (UK htr) into the next st * , rep from * to * around [32 sts].

Round 5: Work * 1 hdc (UK htr) into each of the next 3 sts, then 2 hdc (UK htr) into the next st * , rep from * to * around [40 sts].

Round 6: Work * 1 hdc (UK htr) into each of the next 4 sts, then 2 hdc (UK htr) into the next st * , rep from * to * around [48 sts].

Round 7: Work * 1 hdc (UK htr) into each of the next 5 sts, then 2 hdc (UK htr) into the next st * , rep from * to * around [56 sts].

Round 8: Work * 1 hdc (UK htr) into each of the next 6 sts, then 2 hdc (UK htr) into the next st * , rep from * to * around [64 sts].

Round 9: Work * 1 hdc (UK htr) into each of the next 7 sts, then 2 hdc (UK htr) into the next st * , rep from * to * around [72 sts].

Round 10: Work * 1 hdc (UK htr) into each of the next 8 sts, then 2 hdc (UK htr) into the next st * , rep from * to * around [80 sts].

Round 11: Work * 1 hdc (UK htr) into each of the next 9 sts, then 2 hdc (UK htr) into the next st * , rep from * to * around [88 sts].

Rounds 12–21: work 1 hdc (UK htr) into each st around [88 sts].

Round 22 (hat band): Work spiral rounds of sc (*UK dc*) to create the band, using the yarn double by taking the yarn end from the other end of the ball. Decrease in this round by working sc2tog (*UK dc2tog*) into each st around [44 sts].

Rounds 23–25: Work sc (*UK dc*) into each st around with double yarn. Close round 25 with a sl st into the 1st st of the round. Work these rounds tightly or loosely to obtain the correct fit.

Hippy Chic

Size:
Head circumference 54–58cm (21¼–23in)

Materials:
1 x 50g (1¾oz) ball of Schachenmayr SMC Extra Merino yarn or other soft merino yarn in lavender (48), orange (34), cyclamen (37), azalea/purple (40) and violet (48)

Crochet hook, size 3mm (US C/2, UK 11)

Tension sample:
18 sts and 11 rows of dc (UK tr) using the 3mm (US C/2, UK 11) crochet hook = 10 x 10cm (4 x 4in). Change your hook if necessary to obtain the correct tension (gauge).

Changing colours:
Rows 1–7: lavender; Rows 8–14: orange; Rows 15–21: cyclamen; Rows 22–32: azalea/purple.

Tip:
You can crochet this beanie in just one colour using two balls of yarn.

Basic pattern:
This hat is worked as a flat piece in rows. Work the 1st dc (UK tr) of the row into the 4th ch from the hook. The letter A on the chart marks the start of the foundation ch. The numbers show the start of each row. Start each row with 3 turning ch to replace the 1st dc (UK tr). On each row, start by working 1 st before the repeat, work the repeats as required, and finish with 1 st after the final repeat. Rep rows 1–7 to obtain the correct length, making sure the rows align.

Instructions:
Crochet the hat as a flat piece and sew together afterwards at the centre back.

Working in lavender yarn, begin with 90 ch, which includes 3 ch to replace the 1st dc (UK tr). Work following the chart and the instructions

for the basic pattern, making the colour changes given above. From row 28, work decreases in azalea/purple to make the shape of the hat as follows:

Row 28: 3 ch (= 1st dc/UK tr), dc2tog (UK tr2tog), * 1 dc (UK tr), dc2tog (UK tr2tog)* , rep from * to * to end of row [58 sts].

Row 29: 3 ch (= 1st dc/UK tr), work 1 dc (UK tr) into each st [58 sts].

Row 30: 3 ch (= 1st dc/UK tr), work 1 dc (UK tr) into every 2nd dc (UK tr) of the previous row, skipping the sts in between [29 sts].

Row 31: 3 ch, work 1 dc (UK tr) into each st [29 sts].

Row 32: Repeat row 30 [15 sts]. Fasten off.

Making up:
Draw together the remaining 15 sts with the yarn end, catching in the decrease loop of the dc (UK tr) each time. Join the sides to make a centre-back seam and finish off the yarn ends.

Edging, round 1: Using violet yarn, work * 1 sc (UK dc) around the next dc (UK tr) of the 1st row, pull up the st close to the edge then ch 1, skip 1 dc (UK tr)* , repeat from * to * to the end and join the round with a sl st.

Round 2: Work 1 ch then sc (UK dc) into each st of the previous round; join into a round with a sl st.

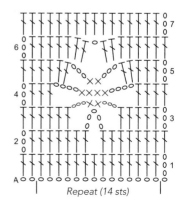

Repeat (14 sts)

20

Dream Weave

Size:
Head circumference 54–58cm (21¼–23in)

Materials:
1 x 100g (3½oz) ball of Rowan Tumble or similar super-bulky/chunky yarn in sky blue (566)

Crochet hook, size 12mm (US P/17)

Tension sample:
4 sts (4 sc /UK dc and 1 ch) in woven pattern and 7 rounds using the 12mm (US P/17) crochet hook = 10 x 10cm (4 x 4in). Change your hook if necessary to obtain the correct tension (gauge).

Getting a good fit:
The size of the hat will depend on whether round 15 is worked loosely or tightly. For a smaller head size, crochet a little tighter (or even change to a slightly smaller hook).

Woven pattern:
Round 1: * 1 ch, 1 sc (UK dc) * , rep from * to * to the end.

Round 2: Rep round 1, but stagger the sc (UK dc) by crocheting around the ch of the previous round.

Round 3 onwards: Rep round 2, always working the sc (UK dc) around the ch of the previous round, rather than inserting the hook into the ch itself. This creates the woven effect. Work in spiral rounds, marking the start of the round with a contrasting yarn.

Working in spiral rounds:
See the crochet stitches guide on the book flaps.

Instructions:
Start the beanie at the crown and work down to the bottom edge in spiral rounds. Work the 1st four rounds in sc (UK dc) and then proceed to work in the woven design from round 5.

Begin with 2 ch.

Round 1: Work 6 sc (UK dc) into the 2nd ch from the hook (see the crochet stitches guide on the book flaps). Mark the start of the round with a contrasting yarn.

Round 2: Work 2 sc (UK dc) into each st around [12 sts].

Round 3: Work * 1 sc (UK dc) then work 2 sc (UK dc) in the next st * , rep from * to * around [18 sts].

Round 4: Work * sc (UK dc) in each of the next 2 sts then 2 sc (UK dc) in the next st * , rep from * to * around [24 sts].

Round 5 (round 1 of woven design): * 1 ch, 1 sc (UK dc) into the next st * , rep from * to * 23 more times.

Round 6 (round 2 of woven design): * 1 ch, work 1 sc (UK dc) around the next ch of the previous round * , rep from * to * around [24 sts].

Rounds 7–13: Rep round 6.

Round 14: Work sc (UK dc) into each st around (without working any ch sts), inserting the hook under the ch of the previous round.

Round 15: Work * sc (UK dc) into each of the next 2 sts, sc2tog (UK dc2tog) * , rep from * to * around [18 sts]. Close the round with a sl st.

Lady Grey

Size:
Head circumference 54–58cm (21¼–23in)

Materials:
2 x 50g (1¾oz) balls of Rowan Cashsoft DK or other luxury DK yarn in dusty grey (542)

Crochet hooks, sizes 4mm (US G/6, UK 8) and 5mm (US H/8, UK 6)

Tension sample:
2 repeats and 15 rows in the basic pattern using the 5mm (US H/8, UK 6) crochet hook = 10 x 10cm (4 x 4in). Change your hook if necessary to obtain the correct tension (gauge).

Basic pattern:
The hat is worked in rows following the chart. The pattern can be worked over a multiple of 6 sts + 2 (including 1 turning ch). The numbers on each side show the start of the row each time. Each row starts with the number of ch corresponding to the st height, as shown. Start each row with the st before the repeat, work the repeats as required and finish with the st after the final repeat. Work rows 1–6, then keep repeating rows 3–6 until the desired length is obtained. Work the bobbles as follows in odd-numbered rows.

Bobble: Work 3 dc (UK tr) into the same st, yrh and draw through all 3 sts together.

Instructions:
Crochet the beanie as a flat piece in rows, working from the bottom edge up to the crown. Sew together at the centre back afterwards.

Begin by working 68 ch loosely (includes 1 turning ch) using the 5mm (US H/8, UK 6) crochet hook.

Rows 1–26: Follow the chart to work in the basic pattern (11 repeats).

Row 27 (decrease round): 3 ch (= 1st dc/UK tr), 1 dc (UK tr) into the 1st sc (UK dc) of the previous row, * 1 ch, 1 bobble st into every 4th sc (UK dc) of the previous row *, rep from * to * to end of row, finishing with 1 ch and 2 dc (UK tr) into the last sc (UK dc).

Row 28: 1 ch, then work 1 sc (UK dc) into each st and around every ch of the previous row.

Row 29: 3 ch (= 1st dc/UK tr), then work 1 dc (UK tr) into each 2nd dc (UK tr) of the previous row [30 sts].

Row 30: 3 ch (=1st dc/UK tr), then work dc2tog (UK tr2tog) to end of row. Draw the remaining 15 sts together with the yarn end, catching in the decrease loops each time.

Join the edges of the piece together to create the centre-back seam.

Change to the 4mm (US G/6, UK 8) hook and work the bottom band in rounds of hdc (UK htr) as follows:

Round 1: 2 ch (counts as 1st hdc/UK htr), work 1 hdc (UK htr) into every ch of the foundation ch, close up with a sl st into the 1st st of the round [67 sts].

Rows 2–4: 2 ch (counts as 1st hdc/UK htr), work hdc (UK htr) into every st around, close up with a sl st into the 1st st of the round. Finish off.

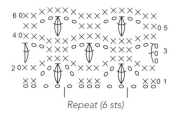

Repeat (6 sts)

Colour Clash

Size:
Head circumference 54–58cm (21¼–23in)

Materials:
Schachenmayr SMC Boston or other super-bulky/chunky easy-care yarn in burgundy (132), lavender (47), neon orange (122), fire red (30) and violet/purple (49)

Crochet hook, sizes 7mm (US L/11, UK 2)

Tension sample:
7 sts and 5 rounds of dc (*UK tr*) using the 7mm (US L/11, UK 2) crochet hook = 10 x 10cm (4 x 4in). Change your hook if necessary to obtain the correct tension (gauge).

Basic pattern:
Work in rounds of dc (*UK tr*). Start every round with 3 ch, which represents the 1st dc (*UK tr*), and end every round with a sl st into the 3rd ch from the start of the round.

Changing colours:
Work 1 round each in burgundy, lavender, neon orange, fire red and violet/purple. Repeat the colours in order until the beanie is the desired size.

NB: For the colour change, the new colour should be introduced on the last loop of the previous st to give a perfect colour transition. In this case, the final st of each round is a sl st, which should therefore be worked in the next colour.

Tip:
To save on buying lots of different balls of wool – or if you simply like a plainer style – the hat can be made in just one colour using two balls of yarn, or in two or three colours, using one ball of each.

Instructions:
Start the beanie at the crown and work down to the bottom edge in rounds.

Begin with 3 ch in burgundy then join into a ring with a sl st. Now work as follows:

Round 1 (burgundy): 3 ch, work 11 dc (*UK tr*) into the ring. Close up this and all subsequent rounds with a sl st in the next colour.

Round 2 (lavender): Work 2 dc (*UK tr*) into each st around [24 sts].

Round 3 (neon orange): 3 ch, 2 dc (*UK tr*) into the next st, * 1 dc (*UK tr*) into the next st then 2 dc (*UK tr*) into the next st * , rep from * to * around [36 sts].

Round 4 (fire red): 3 ch, 1 dc (*UK tr*) into each st around [36 sts].

Rounds 5–14: Following the same colour order, work 1 dc (*UK tr*) into each st around, replacing the 1st dc (*UK tr*) with 3 ch each time.

Round 15 (violet): 1 ch, sc (*UK dc*) into each st around then join up the round with a sl st.

Round 16 (burgundy): Work rev sc (*UK rev dc*) into each st around then fasten off the yarn and darn in the ends. To work rev sc (*UK rev dc*), simply work from left to right instead of from right to left (see the crochet stitches guide on the book flaps).

Starry, Starry Night

Size:
Head circumference 54–58cm (21¼–23in)

Materials:
1 x 50g (1¾oz) ball of Schachenmayr SMC Silenzio or other soft super-bulky/chunky yarn in each of eclipse blue-black (98) and petrol blue (69)

Crochet hook, size 7mm (US L/11, UK 2)

Pompom maker set (optional)

Tension sample:
1.5 repeats and 5 rows worked in shell pattern using the 7mm (US L/11, UK 2) crochet hook = 10 x 10cm (4 x 4in). Change your hook if necessary to obtain the correct tension (gauge).

Tip:
To ensure the hat fits perfectly, even with constant wear, thread a piece of black elastic through the foundation stitches, adjust to the perfect length and secure the ends together.

Shell pattern:
This winter hat is worked in rows following the pattern shown on the page opposite. The pattern can be worked over a multiple of 6 sts + 2 (including 1 turning chain). The numbers on each side of the chart show the start of the row each time. Each row begins with the number of ch corresponding to the st height, as shown. Start the row with the st before the first repeat, work the required number of repeats and finish with the st after the repeat. In rows 2 and 4, the last 3 dc (*UK tr*) of a group are worked each time into the first 3 dc (*UK tr*) of a group in the previous row, then the first 3 dc (*UK tr*) of the following group are worked into the last 3 dc (*UK tr*) of the same group of the previous row. The sc (*UK dc*) in between are left as they are. This will form the stars. Work rows 1–5 then repeat rows 2–5 until the required length is achieved.

Changing colours:
Alternate 2 rows in petrol blue, with 2 rows in eclipse blue-black.

NB: When changing colour, the new colour should be introduced on the last loop of the stitch just before the stitch that will be made in the new colour to give a perfect colour transition.

Instructions:
Work the hat in rows as a flat piece, starting at the bottom edge and working up to the top point. Join the edges together afterwards along the centre back with a small seam.

Using eclipse blue-black, begin by working 44 ch loosely (includes 1 turning ch). Make sure this fits around your head.

Rows 1–10: Work following the chart, changing colour as shown in the photograph.

Now work the decreases to shape the hat as follows, maintaining the established colour changes:

Row 11: Repeat row 3 but at the start of the row, instead of 3 dc (*UK tr*) work just 2 dc (*UK tr*), and at the end of the row, instead of 4 dc (*UK tr*) work just 3 dc (*UK tr*) in the same st. For every star, instead of 6 dc (*UK tr*), work just 5 dc (*UK tr*).

Row 12: Repeat row 5 but instead of 6 dc (*UK tr*) per star, work just 3 dc (*UK tr*).

Row 13: 3 ch (= 1st dc /*UK tr*), * 1 sc (*UK dc*) into the centre of the star (2nd dc/*UK tr*) of the previous row, 1 dc (*UK tr*) into the sc (*UK dc*) of the previous row * , rep from * to * to end of row.

Row 14: 3 ch (= 1st dc /*UK tr*), work dc2tog (*UK tr2tog*) to the end of the row [8 sts].

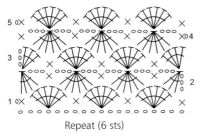

Repeat (6 sts)

Making up:

Draw the remaining 8 sts together using the yarn end, catching in just the loops of the decrease stitches each time. Stitch the edges together to make a small seam at the centre back. Using leftover lengths of yarn, make a bobble in the desired size, either using a pompom set or by working over cardboard rings (see the cover flap at the back of the book), and sew on to the hat.

Flirty Flowers

Size:
Head circumference 54–58cm (21¼–23in)

Materials:
2 x 50g balls of Schachenmayr SMC Aventica
    or similar multi-coloured Aran/bulky-weight
    yarn in wine (88)

Crochet hooks, sizes 6mm (US J/10, UK 4) and
    7mm (US L/11, UK 2)

Tension sample:
4 pattern repeats and 5 rounds using the 7mm
(US L/11, UK 2) crochet hook = 10 x 10cm
(4 x 4in). Change your hook if necessary to
obtain the correct tension (gauge).

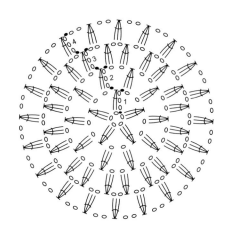

Basic design:
Work in rounds following the crochet chart.
Start every round with 3 ch instead of the 1st
dc (*UK tr*) and join up into a round with a sl
st into the 3rd ch from the start of the round.
The numbers on the chart show the round
transition. Rounds 1–4 are shown in full. After
this, rep round 4 until the required length is
achieved.

Instructions:
Start the beanie at the crown and work in
rounds down to the bottom edge.

Using the 7mm (US L/11, UK 2) crochet hook,
begin with 5 ch and join into a ring with a sl st.

Rounds 1–4: Follow the chart, working the
clusters of 3 dc (*UK tr*) in the first round into the
centre of the ring.

Rounds 5–12: Rep round 4.

Round 13: 1 ch, * 2 sc (*UK dc*) around the next
2 ch of the previous round * , rep from * to * all
around. Close up the round with a sl st [40 sts].

Rounds 14–17: Start each round with 1 ch, then
work sc (*UK dc*) into each st around; join with
a sl st.

Small flowers:
Once you have made the hat, cut off the yarn
at the point where the colour corresponds to
that required for the flower centre (pink in the
example below).

Using the 6mm (US J/10, UK 4) hook, 5 ch and
join into a ring with sl st.

Round 1 (pink centre): Work round 1 of the
crochet chart.

Round 2 (deep pink petals): Cut the yarn and
find a length in the colour you want for the
petals. For each petal, work under a 2-ch of the
previous round: * 1 sc (*UK dc*), 2 ch, cluster of 3
dc (*UK tr*), 2 ch, 1 sc (*UK dc*) * , rep from * to *
another 4 times. Close up the round with a sl st.

Large flowers:
Use yarn from the ball in the required colour.

Using the 6mm (US J/10, UK 4) hook, 5 ch in
purple or deep pink and join into a ring with a
sl st.

Round 1 (in purple or deep pink): Work round 1
of the crochet chart.

Round 2 (in red or purple): For each petal, work
under a 2-ch of the previous round: * 1 sc
(*UK dc*), 2 ch, 4 dc (*UK tr*), 2 ch, 1 sc (*UK dc*) * ,
rep from * to * another 4 times. Close up the
round with a sl st.

Making up:
Make 3 flowers in total and sew on to the side of
the beanie, using the photograph as your guide.

Colour Fun

Size:
Head circumference 54–58cm (21¼–23in)

Materials:
1 x 50g ball of Schachenmayr SMC Soft Tweed or similar Aran-weight yarn in each of mermaid blue-green (51), fuchsia pink (48), olive (71), navy (50) and raspberry (36)

Crochet hooks, sizes 4.5mm (US 7, UK 7) and 5mm (US H/8, UK 6)

Tension sample:
13 sts in the pattern for round 4, i.e. 4 dc (UK tr), 1 ch, 4 dc (UK tr), 1 ch, 3 dc (UK tr), and 7 rounds worked using the 5mm (US H/8, UK 6) crochet hook = 10 x 10cm (4 x 4in). Change your hook if necessary to obtain the correct tension (gauge).

Basic design:
Work in rounds following the crochet chart. The numbers show the round transitions. To start each round, replace the 1st dc (UK tr) with 3 ch, as shown. Close up the rounds with a sl st into the 3rd ch from the beginning of the round. From round 2, crochet the dcs (UK trs) around the chs of the previous round each time. Work rounds 1–4 once then rep round 4 until the required size is achieved.

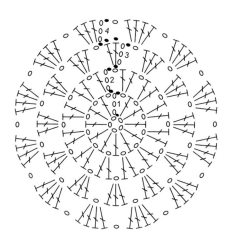

Changing colours:
Work in the following colour order: mermaid blue-green, fuchsia pink, olive, navy then raspberry. Repeat the colour order throughout. From round 5, join in the new colour around the first ch of the previous round. Separate the yarn after every round.

Instructions:
Start the beanie at the crown and work down to the bottom edge in rounds.

Using the 5mm (US H/8, UK 6) crochet hook and mermaid blue-green yarn, begin with 5 ch and join into a ring with a sl st.

Round 1: Following the chart, work around the ring with dc (UK tr) and ch alternately as shown. Start with 4 ch, which represents the 1st dc (UK tr) and 1st ch [12 dc /UK tr].

Rounds 2–4: Work following the chart and the colour order given in 'Changing colours' above [60 sts].

Rounds 5–20: Rep round 4, following the colour order given in 'Changing colours'.

Hat band: Change to the 4.5mm (US 7, UK 7) hook and work as follows:

Rounds 21–22 (mermaid blue-green): 1 ch, sc (UK dc) into each st around then join into a round with a sl st.

Work another 2 rounds each in fuchsia, olive and navy in the same way.

Edging: Work * 2 sc (UK dc) into the next st, skip 1 st * , rep from * to * around; join into a round with a sl st. This creates a simple scalloped edging.

Tip:
You can make this hat in one colour using just two balls of Schachenmayr SMC Soft Tweed. Simply work following the crochet pattern and instructions without changing the colour.

Light and Lacy

Size:
Head circumference 54–58cm (21¼–23in)

Materials:
1 x 25g (1 oz) ball of Rowan Kidsilk Haze or
 similar lace-weight yarn in steel grey (664)

1 x 25g (1 oz) ball of Anchor Artiste Metallic
 Fine crochet thread in silver (301)

Crochet hook, size 4mm (US G/6, UK 8)

Tension sample:
15 dc (UK tr), i.e. 3 shells of the basic pattern,
and 8 rows using the 4mm (US G/6, UK 8)
crochet hook = 10 x 10cm (4 x 4in). Change
your hook if necessary to obtain the correct
tension (gauge).

Tip:
Adjust the size of the hat band to obtain the
perfect fit. Work the band using a 5mm (US H/8,
UK 6) crochet hook for a larger head or a 3.5mm
(US E/4, UK 9) hook for a smaller head.

Basic pattern:
The pattern is worked in rows following the
chart. It is worked over multiples of 4 sts
(including 1 extra ch and 3 turning ch). The
numbers on each side of the chart show the
start of the row each time. Replace the 1st dc
(UK tr) of each row with 3 ch. Always sl st the
last dc (UK tr) of each row into the 3rd turning
ch. Start the row with the st before the pattern
repeat, continue crocheting the repeats as
required and finish with the st after the repeat.
Work rows 1–5 then rep rows 2–5 times three
times.

Note:
For 1 shell, work 5 dc (UK tr) in the same st in
the 1st row and in the 3rd and 5th rows always
crochet the dcs (UK trs) around the ch of the
previous row.

Instructions:
Work the hat as a flat piece, starting at the
bottom edge and working up to the point at
the top. Join the edges together afterwards to
form the centre-back seam.

Using 1 strand of Kidsilk Haze and 1 strand of
silver metallic thread together and the 4mm (US
G/6, UK 8) hook, begin with 68 ch (includes the
3-ch of the 1st dc/UK tr).

Rows 1–5: Work following the chart.

Repeat rows 2–5 3 times but on the final row
(row 17) start the decreases for the shape of the
hat as follows:

Row 17: 3 ch, continue working as for row 5 of
the crochet pattern, but * instead of 5 dc
(UK tr), crochet just 3 dc (UK tr) around the 2 ch
of the previous row * , rep from * to * another
15 times. End the row with 1 dc (UK tr).

Row 18: * 3 ch, dc3tog (UK tr3tog) * , rep from
* to * 15 times, ending the row with 1 dc (UK tr)
[17 sts].

Row 19: 1 ch, sc (UK dc) into each st [17 sts].

Row 20: * 1 ch, sc2tog (UK dc2tog) * , rep from
* to * 7 times.

Making up:
Draw together the remaining st using the yarn
end, catching in the decrease st. Close up the
back seam with a single strand of yarn.

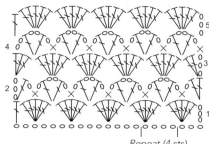

Repeat (4 sts)

Making Waves

Size:
Head circumference 54–58cm (21¼–23in)

Materials:
1 x 50g (1¾oz) ball of Schachenmayr SMC Silenzio or similar easy-care super-bulky/chunky yarn in each of purple (49), petrol blue (69), pine green (73) and indigo (50)

Crochet hook, size 6mm (US J/10, UK 4)

Tension sample:
1 repeat and 5 rows in the wave pattern using the 6mm (US J/10, UK 4) crochet hook = 8 x 10cm (3¼ x 4in). Change your hook if necessary to obtain the correct tension (gauge).

Wave design:
The hat is worked in rows following the pattern shown in the chart. The pattern can be worked over a multiple of 6 sts + 2 (including the turning ch). The numbers on each side show the start of each row. Start each row with the number of ch as indicated according to the st height. Work the 1st hdc (UK htr) into the 3rd ch from the hook. Always sl st the last st of each row into the last turning ch of the previous row. Start the row with the st before the repeat, work the repeats as required and finish with the st after the repeat. Work rows 1–5 then work rows 2–4 again (8 rows).

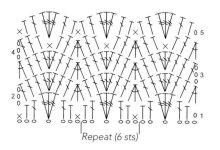

Repeat (6 sts)

Changing colours:
Work in the following colour order: purple, petrol blue, pine green and indigo. Change colour for each new row and repeat the colour order as required.

NB: When changing colour, the new colour should be introduced on the last loop of the st just before the st that will be made in the new colour to give a perfect colour transition. In this case, it should be introduced on the last st of each round.

Instructions:
Work the hat as a flat piece in rows, starting at the bottom edge and working up to the point at the top. Join the edges together afterwards to form the centre-back seam.

Using purple yarn, begin with 50 ch (includes the 1-ch turning ch).

Rows 1–5: Work following the chart.

Rows 6–8: Rep rows 2–4.

Now decrease to shape the top of the beanie as follows:

Row 9 (purple): 3 ch, dc2tog (UK tr2tog) 24 times and end with 1 dc (UK tr) [25 sts].

Row 10 (petrol blue): 3 ch, dc2tog (UK tr2tog) 12 times and end with 1 dc (UK tr) [13 sts].

Row 11 (pine green): 1 ch, sc (UK dc) into each st in the previous row [13 sts].

Draw the remaining sts together with the yarn end, catching in the decrease st each time.

Making up:
For the hat band, work along the foundation-ch edge, using indigo yarn to work 1 ch, then sc (UK dc) into each of the 49 sts around. Work 2 rows of sc (UK dc) into each st. Join the side edges to create the centre-back seam.

Filet Fun

Size:
Head circumference 54–56cm (21¼–22in)

Materials:
2 x 50g (1¾oz) balls of Schachenmayr SMC
  Alpaca or similar DK yarn in vintage-gold
  yellow (123)
Crochet hooks, sizes 4mm (US G/6, UK 8) and
  5mm (US H/8, UK 6)
Crochet stitch marker (optional)

Tension sample:
5 repeats, i.e. 5 sets of 3 ch + 1 sc (UK dc), and
13 rounds in the filet pattern using the 5mm (US
H/8, UK 6) crochet hook = 9.5 x 10cm (3¾ x 4in).
Change your hook if necessary to obtain the
correct tension (gauge).

Filet pattern:
Work 3 ch and 1 sc (UK dc) into each 3-ch of the
previous round, working in spiral rounds. Mark
the start of the round with a contrasting yarn or
crochet stitch marker.

Instructions:
Start the beanie at the crown and work down to
the bottom edge in rounds.

To begin, 4 ch using the 5mm (US H/8, UK 6)
hook and join into a ring with a sl st. Rounds
1–2 are worked in dc (UK tr) to produce the
increases. The filet design begins in round 3
and from round 4 onwards you will be working
into the 3-ch of the previous round.

Round 1: 3 ch (counts as 1st dc/UK tr), work 15
dc (UK tr) into the ring then join up into a round
with a sl st into the 3rd ch from the start of the
round.

Round 2: 3 ch (counts as 1st dc/UK tr), 1 dc (UK
tr) into the 1st dc (UK tr) of the previous round,
then work 2 dc (UK tr) into each of the next 15
sts. Close up the round with a sl st into the 3rd
ch from the start of the round [32 sts].

Round 3: * 3 ch, 1 sc (UK dc) * , rep from * to *
into each st of the previous round.

Round 4: From now on, work in spiral rounds
in the filet-mesh pattern, working 3 ch and 1 sc
(UK dc) alternately, and working the sc (UK dc)
around the 3-ch of the previous round.

Rounds 5–22: Rep round 4.

Round 23 (hat band): Work 1 sc (UK dc) around
each 3-ch of the previous round and work 1
sc (UK dc) into each sc (UK dc) of the previous
round [64 sts].

Rounds 24–28: Change to the 4mm (US G/6,
UK 8) hook and work in spiral rounds of sc (UK
dc), inserting the hook into the horizontal back
loop of each st only. Close up the final round
with a sl st.

Crochet flower:
Using the 4mm (US G/6, UK 8) hook, ch 8 and
join into a ring with a sl st.

Round 1: Work into the ring with dc (UK tr) and
ch as shown in the chart. The numbers show the
round transitions each time. Close up the round
with a sl st. The little arrows show the direction
for crocheting.

Round 2: Follow the chart, working the dc (UK
tr) for the petals around the 6-ch curves of
round 1. Finish the flower after round 2.

Making up:
When you have completed the hat, attach the
flower to the band, using the photograph as a
guide to positioning.

Shades of Grey

Size:
Head circumference 54–58cm (21¼–23in)

Materials:
2 x 50g (1¾oz) balls of SMC Select Diverso or
 similar self-striping super-bulky/chunky yarn
 in anthracite (7593)

Crochet hooks, sizes 8mm (US L/11, UK 0) and
 15mm (US P/16)

Pompom-maker set (optional)

Tension sample:
8 sts, i.e. 1 bobble + 1 ch alternately 4 times,
and 6.5 rounds in the basic pattern using the
15mm (US P/16) crochet hook = 10 x 10cm
(4 x 4in). Change your hook if necessary to
obtain the correct tension (gauge).

Basic pattern:
Round 1: 1 ch, pick up 1 loop each from the
1st and 2nd sc (UK dc) of the previous round.
Pull this as high as possible, yrh, draw the yarn
through all 3 loops on the hook together to
make a bobble. Now 1 ch, pick up 1 loop from
the 2nd sc (UK dc) and then from the 3rd sc (UK
dc) of the previous round, yrh, then draw the
yarn through all 3 loops on the hook together
to make the 2nd bobble. Continue working in
this way until you have made 16 bobbles, each
followed by 1 ch.

Round 2 onwards: 1 ch, pick up 1 loop each
under the 1st and 2nd ch of the previous round,
pull this fairly high, yrh, draw the yarn through
all 3 loops on the hook together to make a
bobble. Now 1 ch, pick up another loop each
under the 2nd and 3rd ch of the previous
round, yrh, draw the yarn through all 3 sts on
the hook together to make the 2nd bobble.
1 ch and continue working in the same way in
spiral rounds, alternating 1 bobble and 1 ch
each time.

Instructions:
Start the beanie at the top and work down to
the bottom edge in spiral rounds.

Begin with 2 ch using the 15mm (US P/16) hook.

Round 1: Work 8 sc (UK dc) into the 2nd ch
from the hook (see the crochet stitches guide
on the book flaps).

Round 2: Work 2 sc (UK dc) into each st
around [16 sts].

Rounds 3–16: Work in the basic pattern
following the instructions above.

Hat band: When the piece is roughly 25cm
(9¾in) long, change to the 8mm (US L/11, UK 0)
hook and work 2 sc (UK dc) into each st around
[32 sts]. Work another spiral round of sc (UK dc)
without increase. When the piece is roughly
27cm (10½in) long, close the round with a sl st.

Making up:
Using leftover yarn, make a pompom about
7cm (2¾in) in diameter. Use a pompom set or
cut cardboard rings to work over (see the cover
flap at the back of the book). Sew the pompom
to the top of the hat.

Winter Wonder

Size:
Head circumference 54–58cm (21¼–23in)

Materials:
2 x 50g balls of Rowan Purelife British Sheep Breeds Fine Bouclé or similar worsted-weight yarn in Ecru Masham (316)

Crochet hook, size 6mm (US J/10, UK 4)

Pompom-maker set (optional)

Tension sample:
10 sts and 8 rows in the bobble pattern using the 6mm (US J/10, UK 4) crochet hook = 10 x 10cm (4 x 4in). Change your hook if necessary to obtain the correct tension (gauge).

Bobble pattern:
Work back and forth in rows following the crochet chart. The pattern can be worked over a multiple of 5 sts + 2 for the turning ch. Crochet the 1st dc (UK tr) of the 1st row into the 3rd ch from the hook. The numbers on each side show the start of the row. Each row starts with the appropriate number of ch for the st height as shown. Sl st the last stitch in every row into the last stitch of the previous row. Start the row with the st before the repeat, then work the required number of repeats and finish with the st after the repeat. Work rows 1–3 then repeat rows 2–3 until the required length is achieved.

For each bobble, work dc4tog (UK tr4tog) into 1 st, then draw the yarn through the 5 loops on the hook together. Crochet the bobbles on WS rows, even though they will appear on RS rows.

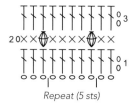

Repeat (5 sts)

Instructions:
Work the hat as a flat piece in rows, starting at the bottom edge and working up to the top point. Join the edges together afterwards to form the centre-back seam.

Begin by working 47 ch loosely (includes 2-ch turning ch). Check that this foundation ch fits around your head.

Row 1: Work 1 dc (UK tr) into the 3rd ch from the hook and then into each subsequent ch [45 sts].

Rows 2–22: Work in the bobble design following the chart.

Now decrease to shape the top of the hat as follows:

Row 23 (RS row): 2 ch, 4 dc (UK tr), dc2tog (UK tr2tog), * 3 dc (UK tr), dc2tog (UK tr2tog) * , rep from * to * , ending with 4 dc (UK tr).

Row 24 (WS row): 1 ch, 2 sc (UK dc), * 1 bobble, 3 sc (UK dc) * , rep from * to * ending with 1 bobble and 2 sc (UK dc).

Row 25: 2 ch, 1 dc (UK tr), then work dc2tog (UK tr2tog) to the end of the row.

Row 26: 1 ch, * work 1 sc (UK dc) then 1 bobble* , rep from * to * ending with 1 sc (UK dc).

Row 27: 2 ch, then work dc2tog (UK tr2tog) to the end of the row.

Making up:
Draw together the remaining sts for the top of the hat using the yarn end, catching in only the decrease stitches. Join the side edges together to form the centre-back seam.

For the hat band, pick up a st in each ch of the foundation ch and work 3 spiral rounds of sc (UK dc) [45 sts]. Finish the final round with a sl st into the 1st st of the round.

Make a pompom with a diameter of about 6cm (2½in) using the pompom set or by working over cardboard rings (see cover flaps at the back of the book). Sew the pompom on to the point of the hat.

Chic Black and White

Size:
Head circumference 54–58cm (21¼–23in)

Materials:
1 x 50g (1¾oz) ball of SMC Select Extra Soft
  Merino Cotton or similar DK yarn in each of
  black (5614) and white (5603)

Crochet hook, size 4.5mm (US 7, UK 7)

Pompom-maker set (optional)

Tension sample:
15 sts and 15 rows in the two-tone pattern using
the 4.5mm (US 7, UK 7) crochet hook
= 10 x 10cm (4 x 4in). Change your hook if
necessary to obtain the correct tension (gauge).

Two-tone pattern:
Work in rows following the crochet pattern
below. The pattern can be worked over a
multiple of 10 sts + 2 sts (including 1 turning
ch). The numbers on each side show the start
of the row. Crochet the 1st sc (UK dc) of the
1st row into the 2nd ch from the hook. Start
the row with the st before the repeat, work the
required number of repeats and then finish with
the st after the repeat. On rows 4 and 8, insert
the hook 2 rows lower each time for the long
dc (UK tr) by inserting the hook around the ch
of the 2nd and 6th rows respectively. Work rows
1–8, then keep repeating all 8 rows but in the
1st row of the repeat always crochet the sc
(UK dc) into the sc (UK dc) of the previous row.

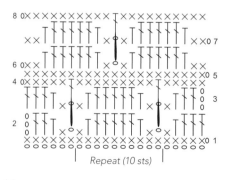

Repeat (10 sts)

Changing colours:
Work 1 row in black to start then alternate
2 rows in white with 2 rows in black for the
remainder of the pattern.

NB: When changing colour, the new colour
should be introduced on the last loop of the
stitch just before the stitch that will be made
in the new colour to give a perfect colour
transition. In this case, it should be introduced
on the last st of the row.

Instructions:
Work the hat as a flat piece in rows, starting at
the bottom edge and working up to the point
at the top. Join the edges together afterwards
to form the centre-back seam.

Begin in black with 71 ch (includes 1 turning ch).

Rows 1–32: Work following the colour changes
explained above. Work the 1st sc (UK dc) of the
1st row into the 2nd ch from the hook.

Row 33 (black): 1 ch, continue working in
sc (UK dc), but at the same time decreasing
every 4th and 5th sc (UK dc) tog. End the row
with 1 sc (UK dc).

Row 34 (white): 3 ch (= 1st dc/UK tr), 1 dc
(UK tr), dc2tog (UK tr2tog) * , 2 dc (UK tr),
dc2tog (UK tr2tog) * , rep from * to * , ending
with 1 dc (UK tr).

Row 35 (white): 1 ch, work sc (UK dc) into each
st [43 sts].

Row 36 (black): 1 ch, * 1 sc (UK dc), sc2tog
(UK dc2tog) * , rep from * to * , ending with
1 sc (UK dc).

Row 37 (black): 1 ch, work sc (UK dc) into each
st [29 sts].

Row 38 (white): 3 ch (= 1st dc/UK tr), work
dc2tog (UK tr2tog) to end of row [15 sts].

Row 39 (white): 1 ch, sc (UK dc) into each
st [15 sts].

Row 40 (black): 1 ch, * 1 sc (UK dc), sc2tog (UK
dc2tog) * , rep from * to * to end of row [10 sts].

Row 41 (black): 1 ch, sc (UK dc) into each st.
Finish off.

Hat band: Work 3 rows of sc (*UK dc*) along the foundation ch. Now work a final row in rev sc (*UK rev dc*) as described on the crochet stitches guide on the book flaps.

Making up:

Join the side edges to make the centre-back seam.

Make a black pompom about 5cm (2in) in diameter either using the pompom set or by working over cardboard rings (see cover flap at the back of the book). Sew the pompom to the point of the hat.

Street Smart

Size:
Head circumference 54–58cm (21¼–23in)

Materials:
1 x 50g (1¾oz) ball of Schachenmayr SMC Soft Tweed or similar easy-care Aran-weight yarn in each of silver grey (90), raspberry (36), lavender (47) and plum (49)

Crochet hooks, sizes 4.5mm (US 7, UK 7) and 6mm (US J/10, UK 4)

Tension sample:
Rounds 1–2 of the crochet pattern using the 4.5mm (US 7, UK 7) hook = 9.5cm (3¾in) diameter and rounds 1–5 = 18cm (7in).

Basic pattern:
The chart for the pattern is given on page 7. Work rounds 1–10 following the chart and using the colours listed in 'Changing colours' below. The rounds are shown in full. Start the round with 1, 3 or 4 ch and end with a sl st into the 1st, 3rd or 4th ch of the start of the round respectively. The foundation ch of a round is made up each time of 1 dc (UK tr) and 1 tr (UK dtr) and 1 sc (UK dc) respectively. The numbers show the round transitions each time. Always crochet the dctog (UK trtog) and trtog (UK dtrtog) around the ch of the previous round. For each puff, work dc3tog (UK tr3tog) in the same st.

Changing colours:
Work 1 round each in silver, raspberry, lavender and plum. Repeat this sequence once more. Work rounds 9 and 10 in silver grey and then work rounds 11–18 as explained below. When changing colour, the new colour should be introduced on the last loop of the st just before the st that will be made in the new colour to give a perfect colour transition.

Tip:
If the new colour begins with a few sts before the start of the next round, always continue crocheting with 1 sl st in the new colour at the appropriate place.

Instructions:
Start the beanie at the crown and work down to the bottom edge.

Using the 4.5mm (US 7, UK 7) crochet hook and silver-grey yarn, begin with 5 ch and join into a ring with a sl st (see the crochet stitches guide on the book flaps).

Rounds 1–10: Work following the chart (page 7) and 'Changing colours' (above), working the first round into the ring. After round 10 there should be 88 sts. Now work as follows, closing up each round with a sl st:

Round 11 (raspberry): Work as for round 6, including the start of round by alternately working 1 puff into each 2nd dc (UK tr) of the previous round and then 1 ch.

Round 12 (lavender): 3 ch (= 1 dc/UK tr), work 1 dc (UK tr) around 1 ch of the previous round * , work 2 dc (UK tr) around the following ch of the previous round * , rep from * to * around.

Round 13 (plum): 3 ch (= 1 dc/UK tr), work dc2tog (UK tr2tog) all around [44 sts].

Round 14 (silver grey): 3 ch (= 1 dc/UK tr), dc (UK tr) into each st around [44 sts].

Round 15 (raspberry): 2 ch (= 1 hdc/UK htr), hdc (UK htr) into each st around.

Rounds 16–18 (lavender band): For the edge, change to the 6mm (US J/10, UK 4) hook and work another 3 rounds of sc (UK dc), starting each round with 1 ch and closing up with a sl st. Fasten off the ends carefully.

Yarn Information

The yarns mentioned in this book are those used by the author. If you have difficulty obtaining any of these yarns, they can be replaced with other yarns of a similar weight and composition, though please note the finished beanies may vary slightly from those shown in the book depending on the yarn used.

Anchor Artiste Metallic Fine: 65% rayon, 35% metallic superfine/thread yarn; 250m (273yd) per 25g (¾oz) ball.

Schachenmayr SMC Alpaca: DK yarn (100% alpaca); 100m (109 yds) per 50g (1¾ oz) ball.

Schachenmayr SMC Aventica: Aran/bulky yarn (45% acrylic, 25% new wool, 20% alpaca, 10% polyamide); 120m (131 yds) per 50g (1¾ oz) ball.

Schachenmayr SMC Boston: super-bulky yarn (70% acrylic, 30% wool); 55m (60 yds) per 50g (1¾ oz) ball.

Schachenmayr SMC Cotton Time: worsted-weight yarn (100% cotton); 88m (96 yds) per 50g (1¾ oz) ball.

Schachenmayr SMC Extra Merino: DK yarn (100% merino wool); 130m (142 yds) per 50g (1¾ oz) ball.

Schachenmayr SMC Extra Merino Big: bulky/chunky yarn (100% merino wool); 80m (87 yds) per 50g (1¾ oz) ball.

Schachenmayr SMC Sheila Soft Mini: super-bulky/chunky novelty yarn (90% acrylic, 10% nylon); 70m (77 yds) per 50g (1¾ oz) ball.

Schachenmayr SMC Silenzio: super-bulky/chunky yarn (50% acrylic, 25 % alpaca, 25% wool); 60m (66 yds) per 50g (1¾ oz) ball.

Schachenmayr SMC Soft Tweed: Aran-weight yarn (50% wool, 50% nylon); 115m (126yd) per 50g (1¾ oz).

SMC Select Apiretto: Aran-weight yarn (55% polyamide, 35% superwash merino, 10% angora); 105m (114 yds) per 50g (1¾ oz) ball.

SMC Select Diverso: super-bulky/chunky yarn (58% wool, 22 % kid mohair, 20% polyamide); 50m (54 yds) per 50g (1¾ oz) ball.

SMC Select Extra Soft Merino Cotton: DK yarn (70% wool, 30% cotton); 130m (142 yds) per 50g (1¾ oz) ball.

Regia Color 6-ply: sport-weight yarn (75% wool, 25% polyamide); 125m (137 yds) per 50g (1¾ oz) ball.

Rowan Big Wool: super-bulky/chunky yarn (100% merino wool); 80m (87 yds) per 100g (3½oz) ball.

Rowan Cashsoft DK: DK yarn (57% merino wool, 33% microfibre, 10% cashmere); 115m (126yds) per 50g (1¾ oz) ball.

Rowan Kidsilk Haze: lace-weight yarn (70% mohair, 30% silk); 210m (229 yds) per 25g (¾oz) ball.

Rowan Purelife British Sheep Breeds Fine Bouclé: worsted-weight yarn (91% wool, 9% polyamide); 100m (109 yds) per 50g (1¾ oz) ball.

Rowan Tumble: super-bulky/chunky yarn (90% alpaca, 10% cotton); 70m (77yds) per 100g (3½oz) ball.